HIGH SCHOOL COMBO

A Student's Survival Guide to High School

"I am a human being, I consider nothing that is human alien to me."

-Terence

HIGH SCHOOL COMBO

A Student's Survival Guide to High School

Mireille Mukiza

First Printing: 2014

ISBN: 978-1-312-28660-3

www.Highschoolcombo.com

Ordering Information:

Special discounts are available on quantity purchases by corporations, associations, educators, and others. For details, contact the publisher at this email: Highschoolcombo@outlook.com

U.S. trade bookstores and wholesalers: Please contact us on Email: Highschoolcombo@outlook.com

I dedicate this book to my bothers, Blaise and David
You were my inspiriations for writing this book

And

To all my extraordinary teachers that taught me.

Fred Amaro

Carla DeBow

Juliene Larson

Mary Murphy-Tick

Larry Ross

Brent Tillotson

Monique Winfield

Christina Arviso

Christina Schmidt-Gillaspie

Tremane Marshall

☺

Table of Contents

Welcome To High School

"Twenty years from now you will be more disappointed by the things that you didn't do than by the ones you did do. So throw off the bowlines. Sail away from the safe harbor. Catch the trade winds in your sails. Explore. Dream. Discover."
Jackson Brown, Jr.

Dear reader,

No one ever said high school was easy. Every day you will face dilemmas and situations where your values and abilities are put to test.

High school will present you brand new opportunities to make friends. But you also have to become familiar with a new building, your assignments are more complicated, and you have new classes to figure out and a lots of new people to meet.

In high school you will have harder classes than you had before, maybe a relationship that going, conflicts with your parents over everything from curfew to privacy issues. Throw in the stress of college application and friends going through their personal nightmare, and you've got your hands full.

High school combo will work as at your hand reference guide to survival high school, because there are no 'magic beans' for high school success , that will require a considerable amount of hard work, determination, motivation, but this book will guide you along the way.

Wishing you all the luck,

Mireille Mukiza

Treat your education like a job

Education is a full time job, you should start treating it like one if you aren't already. For examples, most working adults wake up each morning, get dressed (appropriately) grab breakfast or coffee and run out the door to work so they can provide for their loved ones. Well, guess what?

Your job is to be the best student you can be. And trust me, it isn't always easy. So how can you do your job really well? Just like a regular employee: showing up on time, working hard to impress the boss, being nice and pleasant at work, being a team player and demonstrating leadership, is what is required of you. You can be successful at school by applying the same methods to you education.

Treat your teacher's assignments and classes like a boss giving you a work order or assignments. For example, let's say your boss for American history class asks you to learn how America once depended on Britain. Know that you know he wants: memorize, make a stack of flash cards or highlight your class notes or textbook.

Remember, if you don't show up to work or slack off, you get fires. Same should apply to your education.

Tips To survival High School

1. Do dress to impress
   - ➤ Dress not to impress others, but to impress yourself. Studies show that taking care of your appearance in the morning boosts your performance and confidence throughout the day.

2. Don't procrastinate
   - ➤ Procrastination is seriously your biggest enemy from now on. My best tip to you is avoid the delay. Create a homework schedule and stick to it, write down all of your assignments in a planner and do things sooner than later.

3. Make upperclassmen friends
   - ➤ Befriend an upper-class who can give you inside scoops on teachers, classes and the ins and outs of freshman year at your school.

4. Don't miss class

> Unless you are really sick or have family emergency, no matter how much you don't want to be there, you have to, because it will be really hard to catch up on even just one missed class. So if you can be there, BE THERE.

5. Be on time
   > The earlier you are for classes, the more teachers will respect you and take you seriously. Plus you will have enough time to get ready and get settled in.

6. Find a study buddy
   > Join a study group that can make the most of man-power and can explain concepts you're not getting. But remember: this is a study group, not a gossip group.

7. Don't let relationships consume your life
   > Even through relationships can be wonderful, you education should always come first. To get a balanced

schedule, talk to your significant other about creating some sort of "work, then play".

8. Find out what needs to be done
   ➢ You need to learn and let your teachers know- you have to be responsible for your own learning.

9. New friendships
   ➢ High school will introduce you to a diverse group of people than the one you were used to in middle school. Meeting a diverse group of people will in return make you more open minded.

10. Don't give in to peer pressure
    ➢ A wise man once said to 'listen to the beat of your own drum'. People will respect you more and gravitate towards you if you don't follow the crowd. It takes a lot of courage to be your own person, and to be confidence.

11. Don't waste your weekends

> At some point in high school your
work load will increase, sometimes
you'll need to make smart sacrifices,
like skipping a party Friday night to
work on a project. But if you are
careful about balancing work with
your social life, you'll be able to get it
all done and have time to spare.

12. Reinvent yourself
> If there are things you don't like about
yourself in middle school you now
have the opportunity to make a total
transformation before the first day of
school.

13. Don't forget your family
> Parents and siblings can always
provide some of the best advice and
reality checks. They will always have
your back.

14. Take things slow
> You shouldn't feel the need to get into
a relationship as soon as you get in
high school. Put your education a

head. Relationships can also come after.

15. Don't get in trouble
  - ➢ High school is not the time to get in trouble for things, because if you get caught drinking, doing drugs, cheating on tests or something else idiotic it will affect your college application and maybe entire academic career.

Life in High School Must Know

In your high school years, you prepare- not only academically, but also socially, mentally, and emotionally – for the independence of the years to come. In high school you will find that

1. People are easier to manage if you are friendly instead of bossy.

2. Everyone approaches every situation with at least some concern about, "what is in it for me?"

3. People hear only what they understand.

4. People like, trust and believe those who like them.

5. Even good people have bad days.

6. Everybody prefers to talk about things that are import to him or her.

7. Everyone's number one need is acceptance.

8. Everyone's number one fear is rejection.

9. Assuming greater responsibility for your own learning.

10. Being more open – minded and receptive to new (different) ideas.

11. Adjusting to stiffer competition.

12. Setting goals and working toward achieving them.

13. Having and sustain motivation.

14. Developing time management skills.

Get some sleep

The big schedule item that often gets neglected by high school students in sleep. Now that you are between childhood and adulthood, it will be more tempting to stay up half the night talking with friends, watching movies, eating or doing all the above. But the truth is that your body needs minimum amount of sleep each night.

Your body will function better if you have a regular routine. So set up a bedtime and make sure that you allow yourself seven to nine hours of sleep each night. To get some sleep, consider the following

❖ Make a sleeping schedule and stick to it as best you.

❖ Create a calm environment.

❖ Turn your devices monitor off.

❖ Set your alarm for the same time every morning.

Learn to take notes

Unlike in middle school when taking notes was a suggestion, in high school it's a survival tool. Even if you think that you will remember everything your teacher is teaching in class, I hate to break it to you, you won't. Learning to take effective notes is one of the key points to every high school student's success.

To begin, your notes must include a few basic components, such as the date and overall topic session (class). This will help you keep information organized when you need to review later.

❖ When working with study groups or attending review sessions, you can quickly reference a particular day's notes.

Another major thing to keep in mind is that notes should usually have a definite structure, just like a paper you might write, your notes should have an introduction, several main points, maybe illustrations, and a brief summary.

When your teacher begins to teach, you want to listen carefully for the structure. Try to identify and write down the focus or point of the notes.

❖ Listen and watch for nonverbal clues about what is important.

Get a mentor

Your friends, family and upperclassmen can offer you advice on many things, but a right teacher can be the guide you need to thrive in your education. Besides offering you with advice, a mentor can help you negotiate you club leadership status, education plans and write letters of recommendation.

Finding a mentor takes time and effort, because there is no sign up sheet or a teacher who will hunt you down to be your mentor.

To find your mentor, look for the following

❖ A teacher you respect

❖ A teacher you ike being associated with

❖ A teacher you can look up to

❖ A teacher who cares about you academic and personal well being

When looking for a mentor it important to remember that a mentor does not have to be a teacher, they can be any one you admire. They can be coaches, employers, school administrators, college students and older siblings. You mentors can be anyone who you can look up to.

Learn to multitask

Before high school your life was pretty much laid out for you; middle school was simpler than high school, back then your mom dropped and picked you up from your after school activities and then come time for a delicious dinner that your mom prepared, then homework. But in high school you will have a set schedule and your responsibilities will increase and your life will not be laid out for you.

So to manage your new found responsibilities, you will need to combine tasks to save time, but you will have to be selective about which tasks you combine. For example writing a term people while eating dinner will leave a mess on your keyboard or food all over your notes. However, catching up on your reading while you do your laundry is more efficient.

❖ Multitasking is a common time management strategy among high school students, the challenge is to find tasks that can be successfully combined.

One of the best opportunities to multitask is while waiting (waiting to see the doctor, on the grocery line or waiting for the bus) when you are waiting you can read, do class assignments or review notes and maybe study.

High School Students Confessions

❖ Your are not alone if you feel like

  ➢ You have zero control over your life.

  ➢ Your parents don't care or understand you or your life.

  ➢ You have two faced friends

  ➢ You are around clique that don't include you

  ➢ Peers trying to get you to try things that you don't want to do

  ➢ You are around hypocritical adults

  ➢ You have no money, and no way to get money

  ➢ You have no transportation

  ➢ Confused about what you want to become

  ➢ You are worried and pressured over grades and friends

  ➢ You have a lazy lifestyle

Freshman Year

You've dreamed about what it would be like for years now to be a high school student. You dreamed about the whirlwind social events, but high school would be nothing but hard work, classes, and exams.

Almost all freshman are nervous about find their classes; figuring out how everything is done, making good grades and fitting. Do not be afraid to ask for help and advice.

Tips to making your freshman year count!!!

- ❖ To stay strong, start out strong, keep up with your assignments and most of all go to class.

- ❖ As a student in high school you should anticipate making new friends, learning lots of new things and of course experiencing some good old fashion high school fun.

- ❖ In high school you will soon notice that instruction move at a much faster pace than you were used to in middle school

❖ Now that you are a high school student you should prepare to make some changes in how you think about school, learning and studying.

❖ Doing high school right means thinking about your motivation, self-discipline, personal responsibility and strategies for learning.

❖ As a high school student you will at some point have withdrawn symptoms, where you will want to withdraw from a course. The reasons will vary depending on your personal responsibility, you might think you will not successful complete a course, or it's simply best to drop it.

❖ High school requires you to think differently, act differently, deal with things different (both personal and academically).

❖ While in high school try to be open minded, be willing to try new things.

❖ From day one of class keep up, you can avoid the stress that goes with getting behind by establishing a reading and studying schedule and following it each day.

❖ You should always be aware of your stress, knowing where you stand and being honest with yourself will help you accomplish that.

Freshmen Year steps to success

- ☐ Explore various extracurricular activities to find what you enjoy.

- ☐ Challenge yourself academically by taking difficult courses.

- ☐ Plan the next three years of your high school career, by identifying which AP, IB, or Honor courses you want to take and what extracurricular activities you participate in.

- ☐ Meet your counselor to discuss your goals and ask what resources the school has to offer for students to prepare you for college.

- ☐ Find a summer job.

- ☐ Do volunteer work or attend a summer program.

- ☐ Try to read for pleasure, instead of watching TV.

Sophomore Year steps to success

☐ Take challenging course including AP, IB, or Honor classes. Keep up your grades

☐ Start narrowing down your activities. Begin to dedicate yourself to a few extracurricular activities, and work toward leadership positions. If you haven't found activities that you are interesting, think about starting about your own club. Don't forget to look outside of school at community activities.

☐ Compete in matches, contests and competitions to rack up awards (colleges look favorably towards awards).

☐ Think about taking the PSAT in October. Your test won't count.

☐ Meet with your counselor to discuss college that maybe good fit and ask what you should be doing to prepare.

☐ Take the AP and SAT subject exams of courses you have competed.

☐ Start studying for the SAT.

Junior Year steps to success

☐ Continue to take challenging AP, IB or Honors courses.

☐ Take the SAT or ACT

☐ Discuss with your parents how you will finance your education. Learn about the federal financial aid and your counselor about local scholarships.

☐ Get to know your favorite teachers well. Start thinking about whom you might ask to write your college recommendation letters.

☐ Focus on becoming a leader in extracurricular activities. Run for an officer position, lead a team or start your own club, business or project.

☐ Get a copy of some college application to preview.

☐ Continue to compete in matches, contests and competitions.

☐ Continue to research colleges

☐ Register and prepare for the ACT, SAT, and SAT subject exams. Think about taking classes or set up your own preparation schedule.

☐ Take or retake the ACT or ACT

☐ Take AP exams in May

☐ Visit your counselor to discuss your preliminary plans for applying to college and sources of financial aid.

☐ Set up a study schedule or take a test preparation class.

☐ Start requesting college applications.

☐ Get a summer or part time job.

Senior Year steps to success

☐ Continue to take challenging courses and keep up your grades. Be careful not to catch "Senior Fever".

☐ Decide which schools you will be applying to and add your deadlines to your planner.

☐ Submit your early decision applications. Deadlines are typically in November 1, but check with you college.

☐ Ask teachers and counselor to complete your recommendation letters and school report.

☐ Brainstorm and write your essays.

☐ Arrange college interviews and practice for them.

☐ Send of your applications by their deadlines.

☐ Complete the necessary financial aid forms, including the FASFA and CSS/ Profile, both are typically required to be eligible for financial aid.

☐ Apply for scholarships.

☐ Ask your counselor to complete any necessary mid – year school reports.

☐ Send thank you letters to all of the helpers who supported you, in the last four years.

☐ Take part in "pre-frosh" events and visitations.

☐ Notify the schools of your decision and send your enrollment deposit to your college.

Join a New Club

When you start high school, you will see a ton of organizations that you would love to join, but remember that your first commitment is to school (classes).

You certainly don't want start off the wrong way by spreading yourself too thin. Because you won't have time to do everything, you will need to make difficult choices. Pick a club or organization that you are only interested in and not just for the resume. But before considering an organization, ask yourself the following questions:

- ❖ Do you feel comfortable with other members of the group?

- ❖ How much time can you commitment?

- ❖ What are the requirements of memberships (some clubs consider GPA's and require teacher recommendations)

- ❖ What does the group offer you?

- ❖ What financial commitment is expected from you (some clubs require registration fees)?

- ❖ Will membership support your academic or career goals (can you it on your resume or on a college application)?

- ❖ Are there any leadership opportunities available?

- ❖ Does the organization's goals and value match your own?

It may be intimidating to do something by yourself; after all, you're coming from middles school where all your activities have been the same since elementary school, were you have formed bonds with your teammates. But take a chance in high school and find a club or organization that you've always been interested and if there is no club you are interested in, create it (in high school you have the opportunity) .

- ❖ If you are interested in a club, go to the meetings or introduce yourself to the sponsor and the club members.

- ❖ If you are the shy type, think of joining with a friend, especially someone you know well.

But keep in mind that when you join an organization in high school, the people in the club will soon become your friends.

❖ Don't be afraid to get out there and try new things, even if you have to start them alone.

Explore leadership opportunities

High schools often have organizations and clubs designed to interest or encourage student leaders to come out of the shadows. However, high schools tend to think of leadership broadly, so don't rule yourself out if you cannot be the president of a clubs or captain of a team, there might be other open positions, like treasure, historian, time keeper or if you find that they is something that needs to be done , create the position (that is true leadership).

Leadership is about making a difference, and that is exactly what the high school wants you to do upon coming to campus.

Leadership opportunities are not just great character builders

❖ Colleges look favorably towards leadership experience

❖ When you apply for scholarships, they will base you reward on the list of activities, essay, recommendations and most importantly your leadership skills.

Ask for a recommendation letter

Whether you're applying for as summer program, a job, an internship or just want to hear someone brag about you, you'll need a letter of recommendation from a teacher. The recommendations are testimonies that teachers will provide you with, about your performance and contributions in their class, and school. The recommendations are taken very seriously and serve an important piece of selection criteria.

* ❖ Make sure your teacher is familiar with you and your work. Don't ask someone who does not know you.

* ❖ When you ask a teacher to write you a recommendation letter, provide them with a resume, which will list your extracurricular activities, community service, awards and honors.

* ❖ Ask your teacher to write a letter well in advance of the deadlines.

* ❖ After you received your recommendation letter, write a thank you note and let the professor know whether you were admitted into the program or got the job.

Planner 101

Even if you have a memory like an elephant and never forgot anything or never missed one class assignments in school. In high school you will need a planner (or calendar). You'll be jugging at least 6 classes (including in class or out of class projects, homework assignments, and exams) in addition to after school activities or jobs.

Planners aren't just for grownups anymore! With all the pressure on high school students to cover more material in less time than ever, they need tools to be successful in school. This can be stressful for students who may already feel overwhelmed and stressed by school work and social demands. Planning is also a great stress reducer! Breaking assignments into Subtasks with timelines that help students feel less stressed because they are creating a manageable schedule for each task.

- If you don't already know this, a planner is tool to keep track of your busy life and help you make time for projects or tests or papers that might sneak up on you.

  - ❖ Clearly as a high school student you need one. When you go shopping for

one consider one portable enough to
carry with you in your bag backpack.

If you are not sure that you need a planner, see if
your life matches one or more of the following

☐ Do you have stress in your life

☐ Do you not have any time for the things you
want to do

☐ Do you want to be a more well-rounded
student

☐ Do you want to be able to spend more times
with your friends

☐ Do you want to be more efficient with your
time

☐ Do you feel like you never have any time

Why do you need a planner

- Handy to have with you to write down notes
- Helps you stay organized with tasks
- Able to prioritize tasks
- Planning ahead and setting goal
- Write down assignments

Choosing a Planner

- Size that fits your needs
- Year, Monthly & Weekly Calendar
- Room for notes and goals
- Easy to use
- Portability
- Matches your style

Organization

- Assign different colored pens or highlighters to each subject (color-code)
- Go through your class syllabus and write down due dates
- Highlight or mark important due dates and exams!
- Able to see what the upcoming month will be like
- Prioritize tasks and do tasks ahead of time

Set Weekly Goals

- You're less likely to procrastinate this way
- Help you stay on task
- Reward yourself at the end of the week if goals reached
- Make new goals each week

Writing down Assignments

- Write details, due date and any specifications
- Create To-Do list for that day

Creating a Schedule

- Set aside time for: studying, homework, readings, breaks, workouts (gym), and free-time!

How to use

1. Once you have your class schedule for the semester, block out these class times in your planner for the whole semester.

2. Any other commitments in your life that happen every time on the same exact same time, should be blocked out.

3. If you are a member of an organization or club, block the time you meet.

4. Block out study time.

5. Make your planner a part of your daily routine.

6. Fill in your assignments' due dates as soon as you get them

7. Put everything in your planner (That includes homework, tests, parties, shopping, conferences)

8. Use colorful sticky-note flags to mark your events

Time management tips

1. Make a to do list
   - ❖ Keep an up to date to do list

   - ❖ Prioritize your tasks

   - ❖ Put tasks in order they need to be done in

   - ❖ Put closest due dates on top of list

2. Multitask
   - ❖ Use time when you are waiting around for a bus, the start of class, your chronically late friend, make the time useful by studying , read or making essential phone calls.

3. Put yourself on a strict time budget- you have to set you priorities. Stay within your time management.

4. Stop worrying

Create a learning environment

To have a successful high school career, you need to have a learning environment that is not distracting but calming. When creating a learning environment ask yourself, are you in a place that may actually detract from your ability to concentrate, such as your bed or, in a living room with the TV on?

> ❖ Sometimes students don't give much thought to where they are studying, but if you can't focus, you probably are not getting much real study done.

Get rid of distractions

If you study in the area where

> ❖ There is someone talking?

> ❖ Music playing?

> ❖ Phone ringing?

> ❖ A noisy sibling

Then it's time to improve the environment in which you study in. Think of getting rid of all the distractions, you can simply find a place or just create one.

High School Students Mistakes

☐ Not studying until the night before an exam

☐ Getting caught up in a relationship (the relationships will take you time, affect your mood and also change your mindset).

☐ Not asking for help when you are struggling in school (trust me, no one cares if you ask questions, some might even appreciate it).

☐ Not having a good balance between school and fun (fun is more appealing, but school matters more).

☐ Not getting involved in school.

☐ Not getting classmates phone number (getting the phone numbers will help you if you missed school and you want to know what homework you missed or notes)

Types of Student in High School

1. Prefect Pants
These students do everything better than others and make everyone else look like slackers, compared to them.

   1) They are always five minutes for class.

   2) Never forget their homework.

   3) A 90% is never good enough they have to get 100%.

   4) They always know the answer to everything asked.

   5) Teachers always comment on them (positively of course).

   6) They're organized freaks

   7) Everything is always in perfect order.

2. Prom queen
This student's life is always a contest and they are social butterflies.

1) Dress's up as if every-day is her wedding day.

2) Everyone is their best friend when she needs something.

3) There are artificial.

3. Drama queen
This student always exaggerates the reality.

1) There are always the center of the drama.

2) Everything is always the best or worst, nicest or meanest.

4. Teacher's pet
This student ruins your opportunity to look or sound smart. These students are clearly every teachers favorite.
1) They always sit in the front row of class.

2) Never miss an opportunity to raise their hand.

(Don't confuse with prefect pants.)

5. Gossiper

These people are absolutely insufferable. They always have some information, usually misinformation about something or someone. Never trust them, because if they do it with you, they will do it to you.

1) They are always whispering to someone, usually their new best-friends.

2) The things they say are usually made up or highly sensational stories about others.

6. Slacker

These people can never be found in libraries or an after school programs. Their ideal moment is with a remote control and a bag of potato chips.

1) They are always complaining

2) They are always lazy

3) Always act uninterested in anything besides TV

4) They are never on time

5) You can never trust them with anything (because you know they wouldn't do it).

7. Day-napper
These people wake up and go to school, they have no hygiene.

    1) They are always smelling.

    2) They never dress to impress.

8. Brainiac
These people are the people who are so smart they will read the complete works of Shakespeare, just because they can.

    1) Unlike prefect pants, these people get 100% on a test, on their first try.

    2) They are always in the library.

    3) The idea of a relaxing weekend to these people is to do advanced trigonometry

4) These people are valedictorian for four years, straight.

5) They have the knowledge of a search-engine.

9. Miss Glamour

This person comes to school with the four-hour hairdo, looking like she put her make up on with a paint brush. She never repeats an outfit. Everything and I do mean everything, hair, make-up and clothes, has to be on point at all times.

1) Always looks like a supermodels.

2) Always dresses to impress.

3) Always posing for an imaginary cameraman.

10.Minions

These people are followers and never leaders. And they never wish to know more than they do.

1) They will never have an original thought.

2) These people are constantly doing something for somebody else.

Academics

"Great thoughts speak only to the thoughtful
mind, but great actions speak to all mankind."
Emily P. Bissell

It's not just that there's more work in high school than in middle school, but the topics, complexity, and expectations are totally different. And when thinking about your academic courses you need to ask yourself if you want to earn college credit while still in high school? Then consider that if you want to take AP classes to earn college credit then you have to deal with the homework that will be given to you.

Also when thinking of which classes you should take consider what kind of student you're and what you're learning style is. For example if you're the kind of student who waits until last minutes to get started on your assignments and then find that you're too tired to really pay attention in class, you really should not consider taking any advance classes because you will simply be setting yourself up for failure.

In this chapter you will get tips on effective testing, note taking, writing papers and presentation and so much more.

Come and participate in class

In high school attending class is a requirement for you to be able to graduate, so it is best to attend class every day. Some schools have attendance policies, some give you warnings and others send you to detention sessions. But some schools give the teachers all the power, the teachers keep track of your attendance and grade you on class participation.

You should always try to arrive to class early and try to get a sit in the first three or four rows of the class. This will ensure that you can see and hear everything that happens in class and reduce the number of distractions you have contend with.

But let's be honest with ourselves , you are going to miss class at some point in your high school career, so speak to your teachers ahead of time. That will let your teachers know to give you that day's work ahead of time.

❖ But remember this, after an absence, never as your teacher: "did you cover anything important in class?", because as a student you should always consider all your sessions' classes important.

A+ student characteristics

1. Not only do they earn good grades, they also actually like to learn.

2. They don't miss class, unless they have to

3. They have an A+ student mindset

4. Prepare for class

5. Study out of class

6. Form or join study groups

7. They know that learning and studying effort your grade and they are willing to do the work.

8. They balance academics, work and play, flawlessly.

9. They're involved in extracurricular activities including some sort of volunteer work.

10. They set and reach their goals.

11. They have strong networks of friends and family to help support them emotionally, socially and at times academically.

12. They have a variety of interests and hobbies.

13. They take responsibility for their actions

14. They manage their time.

15. They take time for themselves.

Studying tips for every class

Science
- ➤ Because there is a lot of terms to learn in science courses, concept cards (flash cards) are a good way to learn the terms.

- ➤ If you're a visual learner, concept maps are great tools for learning science, you will also need to study diagrams, some students like to copy them from their text or notes.

Social Sciences
- ➤ Tests in the social science tend to require you to do more writing. The writing can include papers, essays, short answer tests or group projects.

- ➤ In social sciences you will be required to read a lot, when reading carefully read your assignments with critical eyes and make brief notes in the margins to remember what you read.

- ➤ In some classes of social sciences you will have to remember dates, use timelines to remember them.

English

- English classes usually focus on the author's purpose, character development, tone and mood of the author's work. This will require you to think critically about and interpret what you are reading.

- When reading you should
  - ❖ Detect symbolism, extract themes and recognize figurative language.

    Acquire decent writing skills and working knowledge of grammar spelling.

  - ❖ Annotation in strategy that can be used effectively, with some modifications.
- When reading make brief notes in the margins of your books that will enable you to think about the issues you discuss in class.

- When reading mark crucial passages with sticky notes so you can refer to them as you review for tests or prepare to write papers.

Foreign Languages

➢ When studying foreign language you learn vocabulary, grammar rules and sentence construction. Also in foreign languages classes there will be an emphasis on learning about the culture and the people.

➢ Learning a language requires lots of memorizations of grammar rules, verb tenses, and vocabulary.

➢ Modify the concept cards by putting the foreign word on one side and English word on the other side. Cards can also be used to learn grammar rules and irregular verbs.

➢ Get into the culture. Nothing makes learning a language more fun than understanding cultural traditions.

Math

Math for many students is the idea that there are no practical applications of math, but you probably use the skills that underlie math more frequently than you realize, because math is about problem solving it can also be used in real life.

> ➤ In math you need to stay current, it's hard to play catch up with math.

> ➤ Read your textbook and annotate in the margins.

> ➤ Review you notes daily.

> ➤ In math taking good notes will save your life on tests.

> ➤ Use flash cards to learn math formulas and important mathematical principles.

> ➤ If appropriate, draw diagrams, especially for word problems.

Annotate

If you want to graduate high school learn how to annotate. When you annotate you will make comments in the margins while you are reading. Your role when annotating is to interact with the text: you may ask questions, voice opinions, express a reaction, or wonder about the author's statement or character's action.

❖ Annotation is a way for you to note your thought as you read.

❖ It is also a way for you to keep track of what you find significant, confusing, or interesting about the reading.

❖ Annotation provides you with the opportunity to engage a reading in a way that expands your connection and understanding.

In general, you will either write a note in the margins or highlight, circle, or underline text - or use all the methods interchangeably.

Here are some tips for annotations

1. As soon as you encounter the author's focus or the main character, make note of it. This

physical note will remind you what to pay attention to as you read.

2. The author will either support an idea with various details or develop an idea through action and dialogue. When you read information that clearly relates to the focus of the text or to the main character, note this in the margins and underline or highlight it in the reading.

3. When the author mentions a word or an idea that you are not familiar with, mark the passage somehow – by circling, underlining, or highlighting it – and write a note to yourself. What didn't you know or understanding? What is the definition of the unknown word? Write it down in the margins.

4. When you are reading, the author will include an idea that you find provocative, interesting, or surprising. Or a character may do something that you did not expect or did not like. Track your responses in the margins. When it's time to reflect further in writing or to analyze the reading on a test, your notes about various parts of the text will come in handy.

5. As you continue to read more, academically and otherwise, it will become increasingly likely that one text reminds you of something else you've read or experienced. When this happens, make a note of the connection. You never know how that connection could be useful for analysis or essay writing.

Study Group

Forming a study group is a wise idea, but before you form one, know this, studying with a group of friends is not always an effective methods of learning material for an exam. While with friends, you may be more tempted to tell jokes than focus on your studies. But if you truly think that you will have the discipline, a study group can advance your understanding of a topic and enhance your performance in a class.

If you think forming a group would benefit you, follow these tips

1. Only ask focused students to join your group.

2. Make sure the members of your group take the meetings as serious as you do.

3. Make use you have at least a class with every member in the group.

4. Always have your group meetings about the subject at hand.

5. During finals, every member of the group should at least master one study guide to help other group members with the subject.

When your group meets, you should always have a specific purpose in mind. You may want to review your notes or discuss your homework. The purpose can change as the meeting proceeds but you should always focus on class work.

When choosing a location to study choose a location that is comfortable and accessible to everyone in the group (be sure that your location isn't too comfortable, a comfortable place can get drowsy and lose your concentration). Find a place like the library, where there is a lounge. Everyone can gather around a table or grab a spot on the floor, spread out, and have a robust discussion.

❖ Try to find a place where you can bring a lot of materials, where you can speak loudly and candidly, and where you can remain for several hours, if needed maybe for finals.

Extra Credit

At some point in your academic career you will be let in the best kept secret of A+ students, you will be offered the opportunity to do extra credit, even if you don't need to. If you decide to do the extra credit, find out how the extra credit or homework points contribute to your final grade so you can remind yourself of how important it is.

Usually when a teacher offers extra credit, they are trying to find students

1. Who can figure out this extra – tough problem?

2. Who is willing to do a bit more work on top of what is assigned?

3. Who is planning ahead and wants to maximize his chances of having a great grade in my class by securing a safety net, just in case he or she doesn't do as well as he or she wants on a paper or final exam?

4. Who wants to put a few extra points accumulated in the GPA bank?

So if you answered yes to all or any of the above questions, start thinking of extra credit as free money and it's out there for you to take and keep.

As a student who strived on extra credit, let me tell you the greatest secret of all. If you do the extra credit and get it wrong – even if you misses everything single question – you lose nothing, but if you get them right, you have everything to gain.

Save the notes

Do you know how relieved you are when the semester is over, you want to forget everything you learned and throw away your notes. But before you do that, let me remind you that you've worked hard taking those notes! But most importantly before you throw them away, save them because you never know when you might need to refer back to them.

❖ As you move on to more advanced classes, you'll find you need to refer to notes from earlier classes to refresh your memory about certain key points or fundamentals.

❖ Also you may take courses that seem completely unrelated to one another, only to find that some point or issue will come up that you have previously addressed elsewhere. For example if you are reading The Great Gatsby, you might need the information from your history class in the 1920's to understand the context of the novel.

At the end of the semester, label by putting the course title and year and put each set of notes someplace safe and accessible. Consider getting plastic containers you can easily use. If you've been using a loose leaf notebook, you can take the pages out of the blinder and put them in a folder.

Papers

Characteristics of a good paper

<u>Good essay focuses on</u>

> ➤ Be sure to answer each and every part of the essay fully.

<u>Good essay glows</u>

> ➤ Whatever you make a point in an essay, be sure that it is well supported by a document. Use information or quotation from your texts, lectures, and any other sources referred to in class.

<u>Good essay grammatical shines</u>

> ➤ When you are finished writing your essay, read it over looking for grammar and spelling errors.

Tips for writing papers

> ➢ Picking a topic that interests you (when you have a choice).When schoolwork is interesting , you're more motivated and bound to do a better job, so write about a topic that interests you.

> ➢ Create an outline of your paper before you start to write. Outlines are great way to organize your thoughts and to make sure that everything that's relevant will be include in one place.

> ➢ While lots of students start working on their papers just a day or two before they're due, starting earlier is much less stressful.

Start sooner rather than later

When you have to do research and produce a paper as a result, procrastination can be the kiss of death. Everything will take longer than you think it will, papers are usually worth a large percentage of your grade.

Essay organization

Plan before you write. After you have gathered all your resources and you are satisfied that you have the most appropriate information to support your argument.

➢ Introduction

Your introduction can restate the question or pose a new one. The rest of your introductory paragraph should introduce all the key points you will make in your essay so the reader has a good idea of what you are about to discuss.

➢ Body paragraph (s)

This is where you will develop your argument. Each paragraph begins with a topic sentence that expands upon one of the key points made in your introduction. Use transitions to get from point to point, every paragraph should contain only one major point.

➢ Conclusion

The last paragraph of your essay should summarize the point you made and connect them to your central argument it should also emphasize the importance of your argument.

Research

High school libraries generally allows you to conduct computerized searches of what's available in the stacks. When doing research in the libraries look for the following

1. The call number – this number tells you exactly where the resources in located.

2. Status – when you look up an article or a book, you will get information about its availability.

3. Publication date - does the publication date of the book or article seem to match with your topic.

Web Sources

1. Is the writer an expert in the field; is the writer a middle school student, a business that has something to gain or an organization that supports a certain cause.

2. Why does the site exist in the first place – what's the site's purpose? Is it trying to educate you on an issue or is the site trying to sell a product or convince you of a very limited or bias point view?

3. How does the information you have found compare to that on other websites? Usually there is a good deal of overlap, even on very controversial idea, so if you find sites where someone is making claims, that should send a red flag.

Presentation

At some point in your high school career you will be called upon to do individual and group presentations and projects.

The key thing about working in groups is trusting your fellow classmates, knowing you can count on everyone to do his or her part. To have a productive group, do the following

- ➤ Set goals

- ➤ Everyone gets a job

- ➤ Break it down – Begin by outlining all the tasks that need to be done.

- ➤ Give it some bing – Make sure the technology you use is compatible with the resources in the classroom.

- ➤ Practice makes perfect – Your group needs to plan to get together and practice your presentation from the top. While in practice , think about the following

  1. Are you talking too fast or in a monotone that will your audience to death?

2. Are you speaking loudly enough for those in the back of the class to hear you?

3. Do you really know your stuff and are you communicating what you know to the audience. Are you referring to the notes or are you reading your paper? Are you rambling?

4. Do your gesture and move appropriately or are you actually distracting your audience with your movement?

5. Have you stayed within your limit?

6. Have you pulled your ideas together at the end of your presentation?

Tests

Some tests you take in high school are targeted towards one specific reason, however some tests like the ACT, SAT, AP and SAT subject test target your entire knowledge. These tests are usually multiple choice standardized exams, that measures your knowledge of some of the subject taught in high school. These tests a regular multiple questions you've been doing all your life.

* ❖ If you're preparing for a test, study the test.
* ❖ The admission office uses these tests to help decide if you are worthy of admissions.

ACT

The test is made up by three and half hours of testing and one break. The test is divided into four tests, which are always given in the same order.

English Test (45 minutes – 75 questions)

❖ This is a test of grammar, punctuation, sentence structure, and rhetorical skills.

Math Test (60 minutes – 60 questions)

❖ The test is made up by, a third of pre-algebra and elementary algebra, less than a third covers intermediate algebra and coordinate geometry (graphing). Regular geometry make-up less than a quarter of the questions, and there are usually four questions that cover trigonometry.

Reading Test (35 minutes – 40 questions)

❖ The test includes four reading passages of about 750 words each. One is fiction passage, one is social passage, one is humanities passage, and one natural science passage. They are usually in that order. After reading it, you have 10 questions to answer.

Science Test (35 minutes – questions)

❖ The science test does not require any specific scientific knowledge. Taking the test, you do not need to know chemical makeup of hydrochloric acid or any formulas. The question is made up by six sets of scientific information, presented in graphs, charts, tables, and research summaries.

Optional Writing Test (30 minutes)

❖ The optional writing test is single test that is not required. The essay consists of a writing prompt "relevant" to students, which they are asked to write an essay stating your position in the prompt. Two people will grade your essay on a scale from 1 to 12.

> ➢ I recommend you take the "ACT Plus Writing" because some schools require it and while you might think that you do not need it, you might later decide to apply to a school that requires it. It would be a shame if you were forced to take the test again.

Scoring

❖ The ACT scores the test on a scale of 1 to 36 (36 being the highest). The four score from the four test are averaged to create your composite score.

Most colleges only care about your composite score.

SAT

There are three sections on the SAT test: math, critical reading and writing. The writing section requires test takers to complete an essay that is factored into the final score. The test will take you 3 hours and 45 minutes. Each section is scored on a 200 to 800 point scale, making the perfect score 2400.

Critical Reading

- ❖ 67 multiple–choice questions
- ❖ 70 minute Test
- ❖ Tests critical reading, diction, and vocabulary
- ❖ Passage reading
- ❖ Sentence completion

Math

- ❖ 54 questions (44 multiple- choice and 10 grid in)
- ❖ 70 minutes (two 25 minutes section and one minutes section)
- ❖ Test basic arithmetic, algebra I & II, and geometry.

Writing

- ❖ 49 multiple–choice questions, 1 essay question
- ❖ 60 minutes (one 25 minute section, one 10 minute section, and one 25 minute essay)
- ❖ Tests ability to identify sentence errors, improving sentences, improving paragraphs

The SAT subject test

The SAT subject test assess your academic readiness for college in a particular course. Taking these exams can provide a path to opportunities, financial support, and scholarships, in a way that's fair to all students.

Individual schools may have different requirements for the tests, but most colleges require that students take three exams. The SAT subject tests are graded on an 800 point scale.

The test measures skills required to succeed in a modern college classroom.

English and reading tests tips for SAT subject test

1. Read like crazy.

2. Study vocabulary as often as you eat.

3. Use a vocabulary builder book or App.

4. Study etymology (the origins of words).

5. Carry flashcards wherever you go.

6. Remember words can have multiple meanings.

7. Practice timed essay writing.

8. Think of several canned introductions that can be applied to a variety of topics.

9. Keep your essay clear and organized.

10. Use examples in your writing.

11. Don't try to be a perfectionist.

12. For reading comprehension question, sneak a peek at the questions before reading the passages.

13. Mark key parts when reading so you can find them easily when you are answering the questions.

14. Note the style and attitude of the writer in the reading passage.

15. For the SAT sentence completion question, look at one blank at a time.

Math test tips

1. Memorize algebra and geometry formulas.

2. Experiment with different methods for solving problems.

3. Plug in numbers for variable.

The day before the test

- ❖ Make sure the batteries are working in your calculator.

- ❖ Check if you have admission ticket, identification, number two pencils, erasers, calculator (two of everythih, if possible).

Test time trips

- ❖ Pace yourself

- ❖ Read all the questions carefully and completely.

- ❖ Cross out the choices you know are incorrect so that you don't waste time reading them again.

- ❖ If you can't get the answer, move on and came back to it.

- ❖ Don't be afraid to guess

- ❖ Bring a snack

ACT/ SAT study guide

When you are studying for the ACT or SAT it's important to remember that the test is simply about what you know and how you use it while testing.

To pass the ACT/SAT/AP you should study the tests the same way you study history for a history test. The test is about what you know and how you prioritize your time while testing.

1. Get an SAT study guide, either as a purchased book or as a free guide from the internet.
   ❖ The College Board provides a free study guide and practice tests as pdf.

   ❖ While you can buy expensive study guides, you can save your money and buy your study guides on Amazon or just search them online (Most of the times the online study guides are free.)
2. Practice test taking skills, making educated guesses and taking timed tests.

3. Get a tutor. Do not think of a tutor who costs thousands of dollars, instead think of your teachers. For example, if you are taking an AP chemistry test, ask your chemistry teacher to help you study.
   - ❖ For example if you are taking the ACT/SAT test, ask the teachers who teach each subject on the test.

4. Take practice tests under similar conditions you will be testing on.

5. Identify problems areas and study them.

6. Focus on what the test is on.

7. Make a study schedule and follow it.

8. Start studying at least a year before testing.

Signs you will pass your next test

1. Psych time
   You might be nervous when you think about the test. Nerves can paralyze your brain, making it hard to recall information you knew minutes before. Channel your nervous energy into "I CAN DO THIS" statement.

2. Homework hero
   Your homework is not hard, not easy, but challenging. If the work is hard you will know how to do the work and you will run out of time them before you finish.

3. Teach time
   You have an easy time helping your classmates understand the theories you're learning in class right now, and the more you teach, the better you understand it yourself.

4. Best guess
   Even if you don't know the right answer, you can eliminate the wrong ones through context. When you come across multiple choice question for homework, take the time

explain to yourself why the wrong answers are wrong instead of simply moving on.

5. Figure it out
When you get a question wrong, you can figure out on your own where you made a mistake and correct it to get the right answer. Remember the mistake you've made in the past and endeavor to avoid them in the future.

6. Hands in the air
You know the answer to every question your teacher asks, even if you don't raise your hand right away, the more questions you put your minds to, the better position you'll be in come test time.

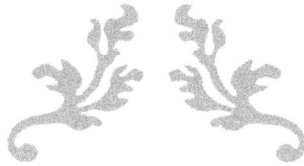

College

"People who are crazy enough to think they can change the world, are the ones who do."
Rob Siltanen

College Application

The college admission process is more selective more than ever now, (more people are now attending college than ever before), and so it's important to make your application stand out. Being noticed is not enough, but you have to be noticed for the good reasons and on your own terms.

To make your application stronger and increase your overall acceptance rate by making your application more personal, remembering to make yourself more unique and more specify to each college you are applying to. You have to be creative on how you represent yourself well.

As you apply to colleges, remember that the college application has many different component including the dry facts on the applications (name, date of birth, SSN and school information), essays, and questionnaire and collecting recommendation letters from you recommenders.

College Choices

REACH

These are your top-choice schools for which you would give up all your earthy possessions to attend. Most likely these are the schools to which it is the most difficult to gain admission. Even if you think that you don't have a chance, apply any way (You never know, it you don't try). The admissions officers might find you to be remarkable than you believe you are (some of the most extraordinary students are also the most modest).

MATCH

These are schools to which you are almost sure that you will be accepted, where you know that your grade point average (GPA) is well above the medium and that have less strenuous requirements for admission.

SAFETY

These are the schools that you are pretty sure you will be accepted to and that you would like, but perhaps not love to attend. These are the schools that fulfill most of your preferences.

College Research

1. College brochures
    College brochures are filled with lots of
    useful information about what the college
    has to offer the students.

2. College directories
    Here you will find out about the student
    population, active major offered, costs and
    financial aid, as well as some useful
    statistics, such as how many freshmen are
    admitted each year. Directories are books,
    websites, college fairs and speakers from
    colleges.

3. College students
    Speak to recent graduates from your high
    school, who are currently attending college
    and ask them what they think of their
    college. If you live close to a college, go
    take a tour and ask to be put in touch with a
    current student to be able to ask questions.

4. Counselor
    Your teachers and schools counselor have
    helped thousands of students get into college
    before you. Trust them.

Before choosing a college, ask yourself

1. What might you major in?
   Most universities are stronger in some areas
   and weaker in other.

2. How many years does it take to graduate?
   Some majors take longer than four years to
   complete, depending on which college you
   attend.

3. Do you prefer a small or bigger college
   setting?
   The size of the college can have a big
   impact on either you graduate in 4 years or
   if you will strive in a small classes.

4. Do you want to live on campus?
   Some students might want to live home or
   rent an apartment with some friends instead
   of staying on campus.

5. Will you be living with strangers
   (roommates)?
   For some people living with strangers can be
   uncomfortable, but others might feel a sense
   of adventure and freedom.

6. Is the campus in the inner city, county side or somewhere in between?
   Where your campus is located may have a big impact on which college you want to attend.

7. What is the weather like?
   The weather issue might look simple, but if you are student from Arizona and you enjoy being in the heat then you shouldn't apply to Alaska.

8. How far is the college from home?
   If you are a student who is trying to gain their freedom, you shouldn't apply to any college close to home or maybe within the same state.

9. Is the school diverse?
   Some students will never have the opportunity to interact with different diverse groups with different kinds of social background. Choosing the right kind of college can open a door to a different world for you.

College Application organization

The college application process is already stressful without having to worry about keeping up with the application, essays, tests and school reports deadlines.

To start: get a blinder

1. List all the colleges you plan to apply to and their deadlines.
   ❖ Use different colors for different colleges you applying to.

   ❖ It will make it easier for you to know what information belongs to what college.
2. For each college, list all the materials required.

3. In the blinder include application form, financial aid forms, recommendations, school reports, mid-year reports, standardized test score reports and essays.

College organization calendar

College organization calendars can be used as a planner or a reminder for the college application process deadlines tracker. Make a separate calendar for each college you are applying to. In the calendar include

- ➢ Deadlines for all of your college application, such as recommendation letters and transcript.
- ➢ Include your personal deadlines, like starting your college essay.
- ➢ Test dates (ACT & SAT)
- ➢ Scholarship application deadline.

Here is how a college organization calendar should look like.

Requirements	Tasks	Deadlines	Complete date
SAT & ACT	Register for tests	Nov 13	Sept 12
College essay	Outline your topics, review your draft and make correction before submitting	Jan 1	Dec 25
Recommendation letters	Ask people to write recommendation letters	Jan 1	Month before due date
School report & transcript	Submit request forms to counsel	Jan 1	Month before due date
Thank you notes	Write thank you notes to all your supporters	Jan 1	After you submit your application
FASFA	Fill in all the information	Depending on the college you apply to.	Jan 1
Complete application	Check for completion of all requirements	Depending on college	Jan 1

Early Action

Early action is a type of early admission process for admission to colleges. This is beneficial only when you have a clear preference for one college. But before applying remember that early action is binding, because a student admitted for early action must attend the college. An applicate of early action must

> ➤ Agree to attend the college if accepted and offered a financial aid package that is considered adequate by the family.
> ➤ Apply to one college.
> ➤ Withdraw all other colleges if accepted.

Early action deferment

Usually deferment for early action applicants means that your application was not strong enough, that the college will re-evaluate it during the regular admission cycle.

If you receive deferment, consider one of the following

1. Start applying to other colleges - you need to protect yourself from having no choice by applying to other schools.

2. Send a letter to the admission office to let them know you are still interested. In the letter remember to include update of your new accomplishments and letter reintegrating your desire to attend.

3. Ask your counselor to contact the school on your behalf.

Before applying for early action consider the main advantages and disadvantages of applying. Also remember to do your own research.

Advantages	Disadvantages
By applying for early action you demonstrate to the college that it is your top choice.	When you apply, you are committing to attend that college if you are accepted you must withdraw your applications to all other schools.
You will find out sooner if you are accepted and not have to apply anywhere else.	You will not be able to compare various college's financial aid package since you have to make your decision early.
Many colleges have higher acceptance rates for early action.	

Tips for handling college rejection

➢ Think of all the famous, successful people who got rejected from their first choice college.

➢ Don't see the rejection as a personal rejection of you as a person.

➢ The college admissions officers might have recognized from your application that you'd be better off somewhere.

➢ Focus on the positive aspects of the school you got accepted to.

➢ If you are still passionate about getting into the college that rejected you, you might be able to transfer after your first year at another college.

Presenting yourself on the college application

- ☐ Do not make careless mistakes, every little thing you put on the application counts.

- ☐ Consider carefully how to strategically present your information.

- ☐ The application is your personal stats sheet. You need to use it as marketing tool. Your stats includes test scores, years of participation in extracurricular activities, number of awards won and grades.

- ☐ The admissions officers use your application as both a summary of your achievements and away to actually compare you to all the other applications. Make sure to include things that will make you stand out of the other applicants.

- ☐ From your application, admission officers will learn about your education, test scores, extracurricular activities, volunteer work, honors, employment and family background.

Components of a college application

1. Essay

The essay part of the application will give you more control on how the college admission officers look at you than anywhere else on the application, because this is the only part where you will not be inputting dry facts.

The essay will be a representation of the person you are, you show the admission officer the person you are, apart from the high school transcript. Try to show an interesting and thoughtful human being.

Brainstorm Topics

- ➢ Think of interesting topics regardless of the specific essay questions

- ➢ Write down all the possible experiences, themes, and aspects of your life.

- ➢ Remember that anything goes

- ➢ Write down every ideas that pops into your head, and do not eliminate them,

until you have finished your entire
list.

➤ When thinking of what to include on
you brainstorming list, consider the
following

1. What is the most difficult or
   challenging thing you have done?

2. What are some strong beliefs or
   philosophy that you hold?

3. What makes you special or
   unique?

4. Do you have any special talents or
   skills?

5. What accomplishment are most
   proud of?

6. How have you changed in the past
   four years?

7. What was your best, worst or
   funniest day/ experience?

8. Who have been the most influential people in your life? Most memorable? Most interesting?

9. What are you favorite activities and hobbies?

10. Most memorable experience you have with your family?

Narrow the list of possible topics?
- ➤ Select topics that are important to you and reflect your personality.

- ➤ Have a unique approach that will insure that your essay will not sound like everyone else's?

- ➤ Your essay needs to have concrete detail about what you have done or experienced.

- ➤ Eliminate any topic that you know will require more than the given space to write.

- ➤ Can you present the topic in a way that will appeal to a wide audience?

> Does your topic involve some insight into who you are, how you think or what you are passionate about?

Answer the question uniquely

> Be yourself
Remember the admission officers want to know the real you. Choose only topics that are truly meaningful to you.

> Highlight growth
Maturity, admission officers want to know you can make the transition from high school to college.

> Use examples and illustrations

> End your essay on high note
A powerful conclusion leaves readers with a strong impression of you.

Redraft

> You will need to rewrite many times to tweak it to perfection.

> Throughout the editing process, keep in mind that your objectives are

1. To reveal something about yourself.

2. To showcase your ability to analyze and communicate meaningful ideas on paper.

➢ Find people to edit your paper for you. These people can be family, teachers and friends.

➢ Your editors should provide you with the most valuable information and suggestions on how to improve your work.

➢ When you editors are editing your work, tell them to look for the following

☐ Does the essay focus on the student and reveal something about him or her.

☐ Is the essay creative and interesting?

☐ Is the essay clear and flows smoothly with nice transitions.

☐ Is the essay flawless

<u>Final essay</u>

> Perfect your spelling

1. Perfect your grammar

2. Count your words
   ❖ If the application asks for 500 words on the essay, don't try to slip in two or three words extra, it will not be acceptable.

> If you plan to reuse your essays, the only major modifications that you might need to make are on the introduction and conclusion on the essay.

2. Extracurricular and Academics

The most important part of your application, are the parts that make you shine. Include things like,

1. Extracurricular activities

2. Jobs

3. Honors/ Award

4. Grades

On the application you will not have enough space to list everything that you have done, so you need to decide which make you shine and standout among the other applicants.

> ➢ On a sheet of paper, list everything you have done, big or small.

> > ❖ Don't forget that extracurricular activities also include experiences like teaching Sunday school, leading a sit-in protest against animal abuse or volunteer as a candy striper at the hospital.

While listing your activities, remember to include the following information

- ➤ Name organization, business program

- ➤ Dates you participated or worked

- ➤ Number of hours per week you spent

- ➤ Leadership position you held and your responsibilities

- ➤ Major accomplishments you made while in the organization

- ➤ Special projects that you initiated or oversaw

3. Recommendation letters

Your recommendation letters should be a letter that is dedicated towards bragging about you. Usually colleges will ask you to get your recommendation letters from your teachers. These recommendation letters give admission officers an insight on who you are as a person, apart from you transcript. The admission officers will rely on them to learn about your personality, skills, ambitions and weaknesses.

Finding the right recommender

A recommender who can support and praise you and knows your strength, who are believable and will not reveal anything incriminating.

> ➢ If you ask a teacher for a recommendation letter and they respond, "What's your name again?" RUN, because their recommendation letter will be dry.

> ➢ You want recommenders who can write about the specifics of your life, provide them with anecdotes and examples if possible.

Make a recommenders packet

Provide your recommenders with all the information they will need while writing your recommendation letter. The materials you include materials like

1. Cover letter – In the letter should include wonderful things you want your recommenders to include in their letters, including specific examples of your accomplishments. The letter should Cleary state the schools you are applying to and deadlines.

2. Resume – This document should include detailed information about your activities, jobs academic and other achievements.

3. Thank you note – Thank your recommenders in advance with a heartfelt appreciation for their time and effort.

   ❖ Be a frequent visitor to your recommenders. Just stop by, or pop in, there classrooms and say hi to him or her and remind them of the deadline, then thank them for their effort.

4. The college interview

The interview portion of the college application process will give you the opportunity to brag about yourself and let the interview meet you.

❖ Remember that the entire college process is met for admission officers to weed out a few deceptive applicants.

<u>Things to keep in mind while interviewing</u>

During the interview remember not to just talk about yourself, let the interview ask you question and ask them questions about the college or the department that you will be studying in.

➢ Since the interviewers are real people, they value real conversation.

➢ Throughout your interview, remind yourself that your goal is to achieve two way conversation. Be careful of any interview where the subject is you and you dominate the interview talking about your accomplishments.

➢ Usually an interview is a two way conversation, so remember to listen to your interviewer and pay attention to what advice they are giving you.

➢ Think of questions you might what to ask the interviewer.

➢ Many students usually make the mistake of not showing off on time or simply just not showing off for the interview.

➢ Some students also make the mistake of not showing interest in what their interviewers have to say.

❖ If you want to look more interested in what the interview is saying, take a notebook and pen to write down any information your interviewers provide.

➢ Since your appearance will provide your interviewers with the first idea of who you are, dress appropriately. For guys, dress simple (no whole suits) but yet classy. For women, a simple dress will do.

Remember by dressing well you will appear professional and mature. Also remember that when you are yourself, you are the most comfortable, the most natural and the most likable.

College Application Check List

Application

> ➤ Every blank and question should be completed. Also, most forms have an area at the top or on the side where you need to your name.

Transcript

> ➤ Forget about any schemes like whiting out less than prefect grades; colleges require an official copy.

Signatures

> ➤ Yours, in all the right places. Especially on the application from certifying that what you have written is true.

Recommendations

> ➤ Follow up with your teachers, counselors and your other recommendations to make sure that they submit your evaluations before the deadlines are up.

Score Reports

> ➤ Get your ACT, SAT, AP test scores send from the testing agency.

No mix-ups

> ➤ If you apply to more than one college (and who doesn't these days) it is very easy to get things mixed up. Make sure that you are sending the right essay to the right school.

Scholarships
Financial Aid

"When the need to succeed is as bad as the need to
breathe, then you'll be successful."
Eric Thomas

There are all kinds of scholarships and financial aid, from money for future circus performs, money for left handed students to money for children of republicans and money that is simply given to you because of your financial need.

Scholarships can be awarded for every kind of family background, interest and skill imaginable.

However, don't count on "outside" or "private" scholarships and financial aid to pay your college tuition. You should treat them as a possible source of aid.

Each year there are thousands of scholarships awarded by groups including colleges, business, unions, civic organizations, churches, clubs, foundations and individuals who wish to assist student with their education. Students can find scholarships in

- Scholarships directories - They list the requirements and details for thousands of scholarships.
- Counselor or financial aid offices – Meet with your high school counselor or someone from your college's financial aid office can give you more information.
- Internet – Find award that you qualify for.

- Local business – As a way to support their communities, many local business provide scholarships for students.

M.O.N.E.Y

Don't ever think that grants and loans are not just for the poorest of the poor, nor are scholarships only for the smartest of the smart.

1. Grants and scholarships
   Money with no strings attached – meaning you don't have to pay it back.

2. Federal work study
   Program sponsored by the government or off campus at a non-profit organization or public agency while you are a student.

3. Loans
   These are typically the easiest to qualify for but that's because they must be paid back with interest.

4. State aid
   Individual states also award money usually through their education agencies.

Federal financial aid

1. <u>Federal Pell grants</u>

   The Federal Pell Grant Program provides need-based grants usually awarded to low-income students who have not earned a bachelor's or a professional degree.

   - A Federal Pell Grant, unlike a loan, does not have to be repaid.

   - The amount depends on your financial need, costs to attend school, status as a full-time or part-time student, and plans to attend school for a full academic year or less.

2. <u>Federal Stafford loans</u>

   Federal Stafford Loans are a form of federal student loans for undergraduate and graduate students enrolled in college at least half time.

   - Stafford loans are the most common form of government student loans.

   - There are many Stafford loan benefits, but one of the greatest benefits is that they are not credit-based.

3. Federal Plus loans

PLUS loans are federal loans that students and parents of dependent undergraduate students can use to help pay education expenses. The maximum loan amount is the student's cost of attendance (determined by the school) minus any other financial aid received.

- The U.S. Department of Education is the lender.

- The borrower must not have an adverse credit history.

4. Consolidations loans

A Direct Consolidation Loan allows you to consolidate (combine) multiple federal education loans into one loan. The result is a single monthly payment instead of multiple payments.

5. Federal supplemental education opportunity grants (ESEOG)
6. To get an FSEOG, you must fill out the Free Application for Federal Student Aid (FAFSA) so your college can determine how much financial need you can get.
   - The FSEOG does not need to be repaid.

7. <u>Federal work study</u>

The FWS Program provides funds for part-time employment to help needy students to finance the costs of postsecondary education.

- Students may be employed by: the college, or local public agency, a private nonprofit organization.

8. <u>Federal Perkins loans</u>

Loans made through the Federal Perkins Loan Program, are low-interest federal student loans for undergraduate and graduate students with exceptional financial need.

- Interest rate for this loan is 5%.

- Your school is the lender

- Funds depend on your financial need and the availability of funds at your college.

Go Digital

"Life is 10% what happens to me and 90% how I react to it."
Charles R. Swindoll

Must have Apps

1. <u>Google drive, OneDrive, Dropbox</u>
   - ❖ These Apps work as flash drives, but they offer are more than the old fashion drives.
   1) The apps are free
   2) You can sync documents between devices
   3) Since the drives are in the cloud, you can never forget your documents or lose them (Unless you forget your password)
   4) You can share your files easily from any where
   5) Access files you saved on the Apps from all your devices
      - ➤ TIP: With Google drive and OneDrive you can edit or create PowerPoints, word document, excel spreadsheets for free. With this you have the advantage of editing papers or checking on your presentation anywhere, from your phone

before presenting or redrafting your final paper as the teacher gives new instructions.

2. <u>Dictionary</u>
   - ❖ The days of buying or carrying around a paper dictionaries are long gone. Now you can carry over 2,000,000 definitions, synonymous and antonyms, all in your pocket.

3. <u>Calculator</u>
   - ❖ Even though you can find a simple calculator for $10 or even free, a good one can almost cost as much money $500. But now you can download a $500 calculator for free from your App store.

4. <u>Scanner</u>
   - ❖ In high school teachers will give countless handouts, and as a student you will lose or forget where you put the handout. Having a scanner App you will be able to scan the document and save it, for easy access.

5. <u>Dragon Dictation</u>

❖ This App is everything that you have been waiting for. Dragon Dictation is a voice recognition application that allows you to easily speak and instantly see your text or email message.

➢ TIP: Turn on the App when the teacher gives last minute instructions when you can't get to pen and paper fast enough.

6. <u>Myhomework</u>

❖ The <u>myhomework student planner</u> app is more helpful for student than a traditional planner, because you can use it on any device and you can track your school work from anywhere. The App reminds you about all your due dates as time progresses.

Helpful Websites

1. English Classes
   - Shmoop.com
   - SparkNotes.com
   - Citationmachine.net
   - CliffNotes.com
   - Online-literature.com
   - Novelguide.com

2. Math
   - Khanacademy.org
   - Mathway.com
   - Wolframalpha.com

3. Science
   - Genome.gov/12011721
   - Chemtutor.com
   - Chemistrylecturenotes.com
   - Physicsclassroom.com
   -

4. Social Studies (A.KA History)
   - UShistory.org
   - Archives.gov
   - Digitalvaults.org
   - Worldhistorymatters.org

J.O.B

"You make a living by what you get; you make a life by what you give."
Winston Churchill

In high school, everything costs more. Your school activities, sports, clubs, teams have dues, equipment, costumes, and other expenses that allowance, selling candy and other fund-raisers don't cover. Your prom tickets, class trips, car insurance, car repairs and gas. Plus clothes, dates and many more come at cost.

At some point in your high school career you will think of getting a job (not a career) to start earning a little extra cash to cover some ground. But before you start working you would have to consider if it's the right move for you and your high school career. Before getting a job, think carefully about your reasons for getting a job and how important those reasons are. Consider the following

> ➢ Will working produce low grades
> When you work, you will have less time to do your homework, study for tests and get a good night dress.

> ➢ You will have less time for friends and school activities
> Clearly, working will leave you with less time for everything in life, especial with social time.

Resume Tips

The objective of your resume is to unleash your accomplishments and qualifications to the employers committee. Even if you haven't worked, you can create a resume by including your volunteer activities, unpaid jobs and any special awards you have won.

1. Writing your resume with active verbs

2. Highlight your skills and objectives

3. Education. You can almost guarantee the interviewer is going to be looking at the bottom of your resume to find out if you have the credentials for the position requires. If you don't hold the minimum level of education or certifications for the position, consider yourself weeded out.

4. Be specific about your profession background. If you are an experienced person, mention your tenure with pervious employers; and in case you are a fresher, define your professional qualifications.

5. Keywords/Core strength. Most recruiters will scan a bulleted keyword section at the top of your resume to find matching keywords from the position they are trying to fills, make sure your resume includes the most relevant keywords, and put this section at the top of your resume. Don't make the interview go search for it.

6. If your CV is targeted towards a specific career path or employer, then you must know all their requirement and mention them in your capabilities match those qualities.

7. Include your contact details

8. Be professional, concise, brief and clean. Avoid from being too flashy with resume design.

9. Don't forget about branding. Branding your resume is important to proving you're the

perfect fit for an opening. You need to think about what makes you unique as a candidate. What can you offer that others can't? Show the employer you can offer them value and benefit that others cannot.

10. Last but not the least, be sure to edit and re-edit you resume once you are done with it.

Tips To Get Hired

1. Spruce up your resume
   * ❖ Your resume will be the first thing to be seen by the prospective employers.
   * ❖ Make it as presentable as possible.
   * ❖ It's the first impression before the interview.
2. Dress Professionally
   * ❖ No midriff shirts, low-cut blouses, or flip-flops because you are not going to the beach, but to a job interview.
3. Make sure you are well groomed
   * ❖ Don't look as though you just rolled out of bed and couldn't brother to take care of basic personal hygiene.
   * ❖ As an employee, you will be are reflection of the company and no customer wants to do business with an unkempt person.
4. Be aware of your body language
   * ❖ A firm handshake at the start of the interview shows you are self-confident.
   * ❖ Maintain eye contact, stay relaxed and attentive to the interviewer.

❖ Think before you answer questions from the interview.

❖ Don't ramble and keep the conversation on the topic.

Tips to keep your job

1. Always be early

2. Don't be the first one out the door

3. Don't bring your personal life to the job

4. Be enthusiastic

5. Do what you're supposed to do and then more.

Top Interview Questions

1. <u>Can you tell me something about yourself?</u>
    - ❖ Answers should support your career goals. Something relevant about your qualifications and employment history.
        - ➢ TIP: Don't talk about your personal life.

2. <u>What are your strength?</u>
    - ❖ Talk about points that would help you do the job you are applying for
    - ❖ Be prepared
    - ❖ Which skills did you develop as a student, such as, voluntary work, team player and research information?

3. <u>How do you handle stress pressure?</u>
    - ❖ Be honest and direct, but avoid being anxious.
    - ❖ Stay calm and relaxed, because the interviewer in observing you.

4. <u>What do you know about our company?</u>
    - ❖ Do research about the company that you are applying for.

❖ Know the value, mission and vision can help you make the interview more interactive.

❖ If you do not know, be honest but do not say that you do not know, instead say ask the interviewer to tell you about the company.

High School
Bucket Lists

*"I urge you to please notice when you are happy,
and exclaim or murmur or think at some point,
'If this isn't nice, I don't know what is.'"*
Kurt Vonnegut (Jr.)

General High School Bucket List

☐ Make new friends

☐ Finalize your summer plans

☐ Read a book

☐ Ace your finals

☐ Make a time capsule

☐ Have a yard sale

☐ Make a scrapbook

☐ Teach yourself a new skill

☐ Talk to your crush

☐ Volunteer at the same place once a week for a year

☐ Start a club

☐ Clean out your closet

☐ Have a fundraise to support an organization

- ☐ Freshen up your wardrobe

- ☐ Apply for a job

- ☐ Do something remarkable

- ☐ Start a workout routine

- ☐ Conquer one fear you have

- ☐ Make a school playlist

- ☐ Plan an end of the school year party

- ☐ Take a selfie with a famous person

- ☐ Do something extra ordinary for a strange

- ☐ Get straight A's for a semester

- ☐ Take four AP classes for a year

- ☐ Watch TEDtalks for a month

- ☐ Read a self-help book

Freshmen Year

☐ Wear your school's colors to a game

☐ Order a large pizza at 3AM

☐ Pull an all nighter

☐ Get your name in the school paper

☐ Speak to a lunch lady

☐ Wear miss matched shoes to school

☐ Join a club

☐ Go hiking

☐ Go to a theater production

☐ Talk to a random person

☐ Met a foreign person

☐ Participate in one campus event

☐ Go to a school dance

☐ Take a selfie with a teacher

☐ Do the doughie in public

☐ DJ a party

☐ Sleep all day

☐ Have a water balloon fight

☐ Have a pizza party with friends

Sophomore Year

- ☐ Start your own club

- ☐ Enlist in a fitness challenge

- ☐ Go to homecoming

- ☐ Learn to cook a fancy recipe

- ☐ Learn to order pizza in a foreign language

- ☐ Run 1 ½ for a month

- ☐ Have an ideal day

- ☐ Join a spot

- ☐ Pursue your passion hobby

- ☐ Connect with your middle school teacher

- ☐ Start vlogging

- ☐ Have a fancy breakfast in bed

- ☐ Have a movie marathon day

☐ Correct cards

☐ Pay it forward

☐ Audition to be your school's mascot

☐ Have a pillow fight

☐ Go camping in the backyard

☐ Start a writing journal

☐ Practice yoga

Junior Year

- ☐ Start your own business

- ☐ Visit a museum

- ☐ Run a 5k

- ☐ Get a new hairstyle

- ☐ Read one book from the New York Times Bestseller List

- ☐ Audition for a role in a campus theater production

- ☐ Have a picnic

- ☐ Surprise someone on their birthdays

- ☐ Dye your hair

- ☐ Go vegan or vegetarian for a week

- ☐ Enter a business competition

- ☐ Have a day of free hugs to classmates

☐ Write for the campus newspaper

☐ Pass a note in class

☐ Pull an all nighter

☐ Volunteer

☐ Get licensed in something

☐ Learn to develop pictures

☐ Watch a foreign movie, with no subtitles

Senior Year

☐ Register to vote

☐ Say "YES" to everything for one day

☐ Make a sincere apology to someone you hunt during your high school career

☐ Wear something bold

☐ Create your resume

☐ Go 24 hours without internet, phone or TV

☐ Write a letter to a teacher

☐ Host a "senior" movie marathon with friends

☐ Buy a college sweatshirt from the school will attend

☐ Tell your favorite teacher how much they meant to you

☐ Train for and run a 10K

☐ Go a day without creating any waste

☐ See a band you've never heard before play

☐ Go to a football game at your school

☐ Go to prom

☐ Ask someone you've never talked to (but always been interested in) to sign your yearbook

☐ Write a thank you notes to everyone (teachers, classmates, friends and siblings) who supported you for the past four years.

Summer

- ☐ Have a photo-shoot

- ☐ Have a water balloon fight

- ☐ Have a picnic

- ☐ Watch the sunset

- ☐ Watch the sunrise

- ☐ Visit an amusement park or carnival

- ☐ Have a bonfire on the beach

- ☐ Fall asleep under the stars

- ☐ Go on a road trip

- ☐ Go fishing

- ☐ Go horseback riding

- ☐ Go swimming at night

- ☐ Go to a zoo

- ☐ Watch fireworks

- ☐ Play laser tag

- ☐ Fly a kite

- ☐ Go for a bike ride

- ☐ Have a board game night

- ☐ Cook an entire meal from scratch

- ☐ Have a slumber party

- ☐ Learn to sew

- ☐ Turn a pair of white canvas sneakers in to a graffiti memory board of your summer

- ☐ Have a dance party in your bedroom, alone

- ☐ Play spin the bottle

- ☐ Dye your hair a crazy color

- ☐ Go to a concert

- ☐ Take pictures in a photo booth

- ☐ Write a letter to your future self

- ☐ Pull an all nighter

- ☐ Read for pressure

- ☐ Volunteer at a local charity

- ☐ Mentor someone younger than you

- ☐ Ask a senior citizen about their teenage years

- ☐ Go to a farmers market

- ☐ Climb a tree

- ☐ Go on a road trip with no destination in mind

- ☐ Play tennis

- ☐ Take a photo every day of summer

- ☐ Dance in the rain

- ☐ Write a short story

- ☐ Do a cover song and upload it to YouTube

- ☐ Call a random number and talk for a least 10 minutes

- ☐ Do a random act of kindness

- ☐ Photo bomb somebody

- ☐ Watch Disney movies all day with your family (parents and siblings)

- ☐ Create a photo journal

- ☐ Leave a king message on someone's car window

- ☐ Ride a roller coaster

- ☐ Laugh so hard, you cry

- ☐ Watch a black and white classic movie

- ☐ Learn how to change oil in a car

- ☐ Play paintball

- ☐ Do something scare

- ☐ Dance with no music on

Senior Year &
After High School

"If we treat people as they are, we make them worse. If we treat people as they ought to be, we help them become what they are capable of becoming."
Johann Wolfgang von Goethe

Three ways to make your final day fabulous

1. Make plans for summer
   Hours of sitting around and day-long movie marathons may seem tempting now, but after a week, all that stuff will seem seriously boring. Plan ahead and figure out how you are going to fill your lazy days. Find a summer camp where you can volunteer or organize a sport league with friends.
2. Throw an end of the year party
   If boring school days are getting you down, add some excitement by throwing an end of the year party. Get your friends involved and plan anything from an outdoor movie with your family projector to pizza by the pool.
3. Study hard for finals
   One of the biggest causes of end of the year blues can be final exams. Leave school on good note by aching your tests and making your teachers proud. Use whatever you need to succeed.

Brag about yourself

Let's be honest, in the past four years you have worked hard and now it's time to brag about how great you are and all the wonderful things you accomplished.

A brag sheet can be a resume, which lists everything you have done outside of your classroom- after school, on the weekends, and during summer or simply anything you done outside of the classroom that was not graded.

In your list, you can include extracurricular, summer experiences, internships, employment, community service, and athletics in which you have participated or achieved, as well as hobbies and interests that you have.

In your brag sheet include a column listing the hours per week and years dedicated to each activity. Keep your brag sheet on computer or on any digital storage, so you can be able to update it anytime.

Brag sheets can be used for more than giving you butterflies, they are great to have on hand when applying for internships, college, scholarships and awards.

Keep in touch

Here's some news, no matter what you tell yourself your life and relationships will never be the same after high school.

After high school you are going to find that you do not spend the same amount of time with your high school BBFs as you used to and as you move on to your college academic career you will find that you are no longer in contact with your teachers.

❖ Keeping in touch with particular people from high school can be specifically beneficial to you.

Teachers from high school can serve as references for jobs or scholarships. They can also serve as mentors and advisors and they are often happy to do so.

Teachers or friends can help with a direct job search, provide networking opportunities, and perhaps even collaborate on research projects.

These relationships are well worth maintaining. Send an email to a teacher or a friend and inquire how her / his life is going.

Reflect

This might sound either stupid or childish, but granted you've been in high school for a while, and your life has certainly changed.

So to reflect on how your life has changed from middle school, lie on your bed at home and think about how everything is different now, and reflect on the new person you've become.

When reflecting ask yourself; Is there anything you would like to have done differently? What are you most looking forward to in the future? Do you have any advice for you old self?

Spend some time looking through old yearbooks and photo album to see how you have grown up in the past couple years, and when you are done reflect on behalf of your future self.

Think of what you future self might want to see, when they look in the photo album a couple years from today and what they might think of you.

Thank your high school teachers

High school might seem like a distant memory to you now that you have your entire future ahead of you, but try not to forget the people who got you were you are now. You should revisit your high school memories and thank your teachers because high school was four years of hard work, determination and support from your teachers that got you into college.

To thank your teachers either

- ❖ Write a thank you note

- ❖ Visit them in person

    College breaks often start earlier and end later than high school ones, so if you have some time before you go off to college, round up some of your high school buddies and pay a visit to your favorite high school teachers.

    - ➢ Go and thank them for all the help they provides you as a high school student.

Thank everyone who helped you, like: coaches, mentors, guidance counselors, and family members. That might make their day ☺

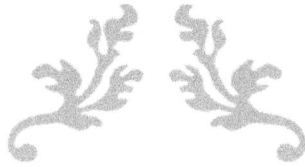

Friendly Recipes

"Perfection is not attainable, but if we chase
perfection we can catch excellence."
Vince Lombardi

The idea of preparing a meal might seem so alien to high school students, especially when most students come home to a cooked meal and they never really have to learn to cook. But we all have to grow up soon or later and it might be saver sooner than later.

So in this chapter I will teach you're a few simple recipes that anyone can handle. From simple crisp French fries and a grilled cheese sandwich to a green salad.

With every recipe I will provide you with the servings in the recipe and step by step instructions on how to prepare the recipe.

The recipes are fool proof if you know and have the ingredients.

Green Salad

Serves 4 to 6

1 small head romaine lettuce

1 small head Boston lettuce

½ bunch fresh spinach (about 6 ounces)

1 small head radicchio

½ red bell pepper

2 small carrots

2 stalks celery

2 ripe tomatoes

Salt and black pepper

1. Fill a clean sink with fresh cold water

2. Tear off the leaves of the romaine and the Boston lettuce, the spinach, and the radicchio and drop them into the water. Let them soak for a few minutes, gently moving them around with your hands to help dislodge any dirt.

3. Lift the leaves out of the water and put into a colander to drain.

4. Refill the sink and repeat this step at least once more. Using a salad spinner or towel paper to dry salad.

5. Wash the bell pepper. Remove the seeds and veins. Chop into small pieces and set aside.

6. Wash and peel the carrots and cut them into thin slices.

7. Wash the celery and cut into thin slices.

8. Wash the tomatoes; cut out the stem circle at the top and discard. Cut the tomatoes into wedges.

9. To assemble the salad, tear all the greens into bite size pieces; do not cut them. Put the greens in a large serving bowl. Add the bell pepper, carrots, celery, and tomatoes. Toss well to combine. Cover with a clean damp cloth and chill until it's ready to serve.

10. When you are ready to serve the salad, pick which salad dressing you would like to use. Pour the dressing over the salad. Add salt and pepper and toss well and them serve immediately.

Black Bean Soup

Serves 4 to 6

2 cups cooked black beans

2 cups cold tap water, homemade chicken broth or canned low – sodium chicken broth

1 hard boil egg

1 small bunch cilantro

4 to 5 slices bacon (optional)

1 ½ teaspoons salt

1. Place 1 cup of the cooked beans in a blender. Add 1 cup of the water.

2. Blend on high speed for 2 to 3 seconds, until the beans have the consistency of thick cream. Some whole beans should remain.

3. Pour the blended beans into a large saucepan.

4. Pour the remaining cup of beans and remaining 1 cup water into the blender and blend at high speed for 30 seconds or until the consistency of thick cream. Add to the saucepan and set aside.

5. Peel the hard-boiled egg, finely chop it and set aside.

6. Wash the cilantro, shake to remove excess water, and dry by rolling in paper towels. Coarsely chop and set aside.

7. If you are using the bacon , place the strips in a flying pan over medium – high heat and fry for about 3 minutes on each side or until just crispy.

8. Remove the bacon form the pan, lay on paper towels to drain, and let cool.

9. Cut the strips into small pieces and set aside

10. Set the saucepan with the soup over medium heat. Add the salt and bring the soup to a simmer, stirring frequently as it cooks. Using a metal spoon, skim off any foam or impurities that rise to the surface.

11. Cook for 35 minutes at a gentle simmer.

12. Serve hot and garnish with the chopped egg, cilantro and bacon bits.

Po-Boy Sandwich

Serves 2

1 small head lettuce

2 ripe tomatoes

12 inch French, Portuguese, or sub roll

¼ cup mayonnaise

¼ cup creole mustard or whole grain mustard

Tabasco sauce

8 ounce smoked ham, thinly sliced

4 ounces of sliced Swiss cheese

Sweet or dill pickle slices

1. Preheat the oven to 350

2. Remove any dark or discolored leaves from the outside of the head of lettuce. Cut the head of the lettuce in half and wash cold water

3. Beginning at one end, slice the lettuce into very thin strips, the thinner the better.

4. Place in a medium size bowl and set aside.

5. Wash the tomatoes; remove the stem circle from the top and discard. Cut the tomatoes into thin slices and set aside.

6. Slice the French roll in half lengthwise, being careful not to cut all the way through the roll. It should fold open like a book.

7. Place the roll on a baking sheet cut side up. Bake for about 10 minutes until the crust is crispy.

8. Remove the roll and spread both halves with the mayonnaise and mustard.

9. Add some dashes of tabasco to each half, according to your taste.

10. Layer the ham slice on one half of the roll.

11. Layer the cheese slices on top.

12. Layer the tomato slice on top.

13. Layer the lettuce, then the pickle slides on top.

14. Fold the top over to close.

Grilled Cheese Sandwich

Serves 4

8 slices whole wheat, white, or sourdough sandwich bread.

4 ounces sharp yellow cheddar cheese

3 tablespoons milk

3 tablespoons salted butter, melted

1. Preheat the oven 400 with a rack in the upper slot of the oven.

2. Cut away the crusts of the bread with a sharp knife. Lay four slices on a small baking sheet.

3. Using the largest holes of a grater, grater the cheddar cheese into small bowl. Add the milk and combine.

4. Butter the top of each slice of bread with a pastry brush. Turn the bread over so the buttered side is down.

5. Spoon one quarter of the cheese mixture on top of each slice of bread and cover with the remaining slices of bread.

6. With a pastry, butter the top slices.

7. Place the baking sheet in the oven and bake the sandwiches for 10 to 15 minutes, until the cheese melts and the bread just begins to brown.

8. Turn the oven to broil. Brown the sandwiches under the broiler for 1 minutes on each side. (If necessary, reshape the sandwiches with a spatula after you turn them, tapping in the sides like a desk of cards). Be careful not to let them burn.

9. With a spatula, lift the finished sandwiches from the baking sheet to a serving dish. Let them cool for a moment, cut into halves, and serve hot.

Mac and Cheese

Serves 6

2 tablespoons salted butter

1 pound extra sharp Vermont cheddar

8 ounces elbow macaroni

1 ¾ cups whole milk

¾ cup whole milk cottage cheese

¼ cup light cream

1 teaspoon dry mustard

¼ teaspoon cayenne pepper

¼ teaspoon freshly grated nutmeg

½ teaspoon salt

¼ teaspoon freshly grated black pepper

1. With a piece pf wax paper, butter a 10 inch round baking dish with 1 tablespoon of the butter. Leave any leftover chucks of butter in the bottom of the baking dish.

2. Using the largest holes of a grater, grater the cheese into a large bowl. You should have about four cup. You can also grate the cheese in a food processor. Follow the manufacturer's instructions of grating.

Reserve one third cup of the cheese in a small bowl and set aside.

3. Pour the uncooked pasta into the large bowl of cheese and toss well with a spoon to combine the ingredients. Set aside.

4. Preheat the oven to 375 with a rack in the upper third of the oven

5. Combine the milk, cottage cheese, cream, dry mustard, cayenne, nutmeg, salt, and pepper in the jar of a blender. Press the lid firmly in lace and blend at high speed for 30 seconds.

6. Remove the lid and pour the blended ingredients into bowl with the cheese and uncooked macaroni. Toss thoroughly to evenly combine the cheese and macaroni.

7. Pour into the prepared baking dish

8. Cover the baking dish with to layer of aluminum foil.

9. Bake for 30 minutes on a rack in the upper third of the oven.

10. Break the remaining 1 tablespoon butter into chunks and combine it with the reserved one third cup grated cheese.

11. After 30 minutes, remove the foil and sprinkle the cheese and butter combination across the top of the baking dish.

12. Return to the oven, uncovered, and bake an additional 30 minutes or until the top is browned and bubby.

13. Let it cool for 15 before serving

14. Cut into squares and serve hot

Fried Chicken

Serves 7

2 cups buttermilk

2 teaspoons Dijon mustard

2 teaspoon salt

12 pieces skinless chicken thighs and skinless legs (about 3 ½ pounds)

2 cups panko (Japanese style bread crumbs) or plain dried bread crumbs

½ teaspoon dried sage

½ teaspoon freshly ground black pepper

1 teaspoon smoked or regular paprika

½ cup canola oil

1. Combine the buttermilk, Dijon mustard, and 1 teaspoon of the salt in a large bowl.

2. Add the chicken pieces and toss them well with a spoon to coat.

3. Cover with wax paper and refrigerate for at least 1 hour, or overnight.

4. Preheat the oven 10 425 with a rack in the middle slot of the oven.

5. Combine the bread crumbs with the remaining 1 teaspoon salt, sage, pepper, and paprika in a large bowl. Set aside.

6. With a paper towel, lightly rub canola oil over the surface of a 13 by 9 inch baking rack and 9 ½ by 13 ½ inch baking pan. This will make clean up much easier. Set the baking rack on top of the baking tray as shown in the illustration.

7. Remove the chicken from the refrigerator.

8. Roll the chicken pieces in the bread crumb mixture to evenly coat each piece, shake off the excess. , and lay the pieces on the baking rack. Do not overwhelm the chicken.

9. Use a pastry brush to drizzle each piece with a little of the oil so you don't disturb the bread crumb mixture.

10. Bake for 50 to 60 minutes, until the chicken is cooked through and golden brown, carefully turning the pieces over about halfway through the baking. Brush them with the remaining oil after turning. If some of the thigh pieces finish cooking before the

legs, remove them to a warm platter and lightly cover with foil while the remaining pieces finish baking. To determine doneness, cut into one of the largest pieces to make sure there is no trace of pink inside. If the chicken is still pink on the inside, bake an additional 10 to 15 minutes.

11. When it ready, serve it while it's still hot and enjoy.

Oven Fries

Serves 5

4 medium size, russet potatoes

5 tablespoon peanut or vegetable oil

¼ teaspoon dried oregano

¼ teaspoon dried sage

¼ teaspoon ground black pepper

½ teaspoon paprika

1 tablespoon sea salt plus extra for flavor

1. Wash an scrub the potatoes to remove any dirt

2. Cut the potato in half lengthwise and lay, cut side down, on a cutting board. Cut each half into 16 to 20 strips about ¼ inch thick. This is a slow process so take your time.

3. Drop the cut strips into a bowl of hot water.

4. Let the potatoes soak for 10 to 15 minutes.

5. Preheat the oven 475 with a rack in the middle slot of the oven.

6. Coat a nonstick or heavy aluminum 10 ½ by 15 ½ inch baking sheet with 3 tablespoon of the oil.

7. Mix the oregano, sage, pepper, paprika and salt in a small bowl and set aside.

8. Drain potatoes.

9. Lay two to three layers of paper towels on a clean work surface. Set the drained potatoes in batches on the paper towels. Wrap completely to dry. It is important to get the potatoes as dry as you can. The drier, the crispier.

10. Put the potatoes in a large bowl. Pour the remaining 3 tablespoon oil over the potatoes and, with a spoon, toss well to coat. Sprinkle on the herb mix and toss again to evenly coat all the potatoes.

11. Empty the potatoes onto the prepared baking sheet and spread them in a single layer. It is all right if some of them overlap.

12. Slide the baking sheet onto the middle rack of the oven.

13. Bake for 25 to 30 minutes, until the potatoes are brown and crispy. Once or twice during the baking, open the oven and, using a spatula, loosen the potatoes. Use tongs to turn the loosened potato strip over to ensure even cooking. Turn the banking tray one full rotation during baking to prevent burning. If the potatoes start to burn, lower the oven temperature to 450.

14. Remove the potatoes from the oven and sprinkle with extra salt.

15. Serve while hot.

Chocolate Chip Cookie

24 cookies

2 ¼ cups unbleached all-purpose flour

1 teaspoon baking soda

1 teaspoon salt

½ cup (1 stick) unsalted butter

¼ cup chunky peanut butter

1 ½ cups raw sugar

2 large eggs, slightly beaten

12 ounces (2 cups) semisweet chocolate chips

1. Preheat the oven to 375 with a rack in the middle slot of the oven.

2. Lightly butter tow 18 by 13 inch baking sheets or line them with parchment paper.

3. Combine the flour, baking soda, and salt in a large bowl, whisk to mix and set aside.

4. Melt the butter and peanut butter in a medium size saucepan over low heat. Add the raw sugar and stir until the ingredients are melted and combined. Remove the butter

and sugar mixture from the heat and let cool for minutes.

5. Combine eggs and the vanilla in a medium bowl. Add them, along with the butter mixture, to the floor mixture. Using an electric hand – mixer, beat on low speed until smooth.

6. Add the chocolate chips and continue to beat on low speed until chunky dough is formed.

7. Refrigerate the dough for 10 minutes or up to 1 hour.

8. Scoop up a heaping tablespoon of the dough and roll it into a ball the size of a golf ball. Place the ball on the cookie sheet and slightly flatten the dough into a 2 inch round. Repeat with the dough until you have 12 cookie on the tray, spacing the cookie about 2 inches apart.

9. Bake the cookies, one sheet at a time, for 12 to 15 minutes, or until lightly brown.

10. Prepare the second sheet of cookies while the first one bakes. And when they are ready, allow them to cool for 15 minutes.

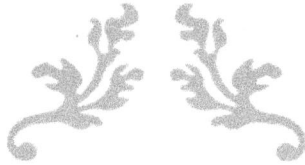

Farewell

"To accomplish great things, we must not only act, but also dream, not only plan, but also believe."

Anatole France

Dear friend,

Thank you for reading this and letting me share my passion for education with you. I hope as you read this that you have at least learned one thing from this book. And if you have, I have achieved my goal ☺

As you emerge on your new journey, I wish you all the luck in the world, trust me, you gonna need it, but I know you will have the courage to keep going.

As you go off to your journey, I must go on to mine and until we meet again

Stay hungry, stay foolish

Mireille Mukiza, graduated in the top 5% of her high school graduating class (the class of 2014). She now attends Lake Forest College, where she is double majoring in Business and International Affairs and minoring in Economics.

www.ingramcontent.com/pod-product-compliance
Lightning Source LLC
Chambersburg PA
CBHW020858090426
42736CB00008B/415